REAL MEN BELCH DOWNWIND

MODERN ETIQUETTE FOR THE PRIMITIVE MAN

REAL MEN BELCH DOWNWIND

MIKE NICHOLS

MODERN ETIQUETTE FOR THE PRIMITIVE MAN

THE SUMMIT GROUP

FORT WORTH, TEXAS

THE SUMMIT GROUP
1227 West Magnolia, Suite 500, Fort Worth, Texas 76104

Publisher's Cataloging in Publication
(Prepared by Quality Books Inc.)

Nichols, Michael.
    Real men belch downwind : modern etiquette for the primitive man
/by Mike Nichols.
    p. cm.
    ISBN 1-56530-054-8

    1. Etiquette for men. 2. American wit and humor.   I. Title.

BJ1855.N53 1993   395.142
                                         QBI93-675

Jacket design by Cheryl Corbitt
Cover Illustration by Jim Paillot
Inside Illustrations by Debra Wilson
Book Design by Rishi Seth

Manufactured in the United States of America
First Printing 1993

For my mother, Susan Bonin
and Jerry Flemmons—
they cross the t and dot the i in "supportive."

CONTENTS

Belche thou near no man's face
with a corrupt fumosytye

Hewe Rhodes, "Book of Nurture," 1554

AND GOD MADE EARL (NOT HIS REAL NAME)

In a nondescript neighborhood in a nondescript town in a nondescript state somewhere in the Midwest stands a nondescript building. It has no windows, no unusual markings; it bears no sign or name plate that would give the curious any hint to its nature or purpose. It is not listed in the local phone book. Few people are seen coming or going through its nondescript door. Most residents of the town, if they give any thought at all to what goes on behind the building's nondescript walls, no doubt would speculate that the work done therein is "nondescript."

Others might whisper that the building probably houses a federal agency, perhaps an ancillary office of the Nuclear Regulatory Commission. Still others might whisper that it probably is home to an agricultural research station, perhaps quietly developing an improved stuffed mushroom capable of taking American party-goers into the twenty-first century.

But, in fact, the work being conducted therein is more important than nuclear meltdowns or stuffed mushrooms. In fact, if you combined nuclear meltdowns *and* stuffed mushrooms (creating a giant, glowing, atomic hors d'oeuvre), they still would not be as important as the work being conducted behind the walls of this anonymous building.

This building houses the National Academy of Gentlemanly Deportment—affectionately known as NAGD to those of us who carry out its noble mission. NAGD is a little-known think tank—funded by government grants and private contributions—that studies modern etiquette as it relates to the human male and, by extension, to those around him. We here at NAGD have the avowed tripartite goal of (1) helping America's 125 million males attain their fullest social potential, (2) helping our fellow males achieve mental, spiritual and physical fulfillment as Real Men, and (3) snagging enough funding to finally buy that fully rigged bass boat we've been dreaming of for months.

Which brings us to The Letter. It was not an unusual letter. Each month we here at NAGD receive dozens similar to it. Most are from women asking us here at NAGD if we can either (1) advise them on how to improve their man's manners or (2) supply them with a list of states where strangling a man with his own argyles is legally classified as a misdemeanor.

But this particular letter seemed to embody, in one twenty-nine-cent cry for help, all the concerns and consternations that women have about the state of men's etiquette.

"Dear National Academy of Gentlemanly Deportment:

"Please forgive me for interrupting your important work. But it is because of that very work that I am writing you. I am at my wit's end concerning my husband Earl [not his real name] and hope you can help me.

"Don't misunderstand—Earl is *not* a bad man or a bad husband. He is well-educated and earns a good salary. He does not drink heavily. He does not abuse our kids—Earl Jr. and Earlette. He does not cheat on me. He has never once brought home a college cheerleading squad and tried to tell me that the young ladies have come to mow the lawn and beat the rugs.

"No, it's nothing as bad as that. Earl's problem is that he is gross. For starters, he belches. Why do men do that so much? Sometimes I think he is not even aware that he has just belched. Certainly he seldom makes any effort to repress or redirect a belch. He also, well, you know, breaks wind. But at least when he breaks wind I know that he knows that he did because he always makes that silly, self-satisfied smile, as if he had just perfected cold fusion.

"Also, he scratches himself. And he spits. And he picks his nose. When he watches TV he picks his nose and his teeth and his toes. Sometimes all three during the same commercial break.

"And as for dining skills, I have found that the most practical way to get Earl clean after he has eaten is to strip him naked and make him walk through a car wash, but he enjoys those rotating brushes just a little too much.

"I don't recall that Earl was like this before we were married. Oh, sure, ten years ago, when we stood side by side in a wedding chapel and vowed to have and to hold from this day forward, for better and for worse, for richer and for poorer until twin beds us do part, I was aware that Earl was not perfect. But I thought he would change.

"He didn't.

"He won't listen to me when I make suggestions to him about improving his etiquette. Maybe he would listen to suggestions if they came from other men. Toward that end, enclosed is a check for what I think you will agree is a generous sum of money. Please use it to finance publication of a book on men's etiquette. It need not be anything fancy. Just the basics. I and women everywhere will thank you. But please hurry—even as I write this I can see Earl sitting across the room from me. He is smiling that silly, self-satis-fied smile again."

Mrs. Earl [not her real name]

"P.S. Could you please supply me with a list of states where strangling a man with his own tube socks is legally classi-fied as a misdemeanor—my husband doesn't wear argyles."

Well, naturally, when we here at NAGD received this letter we were very, very, very, very, very, very (Did we mention that Mrs. Earl is paying us by the word?) deeply concerned. In fact, if we were any more deeply concerned we wouldn't be able to finish leafing through our stack of full-color bass boat brochures.

This book that you hold in your hands is the tangible result of that deep concern. In the following chapters we here at NAGD will try to establish for Earl and our fellow men in general some etiquette guidelines—guidelines for

Real Men that address real situations involving real people. We will answer actual questions about etiquette that we are frequently asked by women and men of all genders.

We here at NAGD admit that we, too, have a lot of rough edges, that our own etiquette is not perfect. In high school we were voted Most Likely to Use the Wrong Fork in the Commission of a Felony. But at least we *know* that we need some improvement. And that knowledge shall make us free. But we also know that as we and other Real Men strive to polish our manners and regulate our gross personal habits, there will be pain, there will be sacrifice, there will be blood, sweat and, yes, ear wax.

Please proceed to Chapter 1 at your earliest convenience. We here at NAGD thank you very, very, very, very, very, very much for reading this far. There. We just earned enough to spring for the optional monogrammed life jackets.

SO WHY DO WE CALL IT "MAN-NERS?"

Welcome to Chapter 1. Pull up a page and make yourself at home. Whether or not Mrs. Earl was aware of it, with her letter she was pinpointing a growing concern in America today. From the lobster pots of Maine to the crackpots of California, most of us men could stand to improve our etiquette.

If you stop ten people—both men and women—on the street and ask them if they think that men's etiquette needs improvement, nine will answer "yes," and the tenth will answer "no" and then push you out of the way.

In all likelihood, that tenth person is a man.

Question: Do you know what the first recorded act of etiquette was?

Answer: Yes, and thank you so much for asking. Ironically, Adam—himself a man—performed history's first recorded act of etiquette: He let Eve take the first bite of the apple. But then, quicker than Adam could say "After you, Dear," Adam and Eve had fallen from grace. They looked down and realized that they were (1) naked and (2) anatomically correct. Next thing they knew, they were expelled from the garden and forced to live east of Eden, in the suburbs, where residents had rusting cars in their yards, the streets were potholed, and the apex of male etiquette was to say, "Pass the sledgehammer, please," while vandalizing a cemetery.

Sixty-six books of the Bible, ten commandments and countless "begats" later, much has changed on the face of the Earth. Paradise is now a parking lot, the fishes of the sea are contaminated by mercury, the fowl of the air are choking on smog, the world has seen leisure suits and streaking, and male etiquette continues to go the way of 78s, Super 8 and Beta.

Adam and Eve Exposed

Question: Would you be interested in buying some eight-track tapes, cheap?

Answer: No, but thank you so much for asking.

We here at NAGD have given the issue of men's etiquette a lot of thought. Mind you, we are a pretty darned manly bunch, you betcha. On our staff you will find men who drive pickups, wear jeans and boots, men who have tattoos, scars, beards and bird dogs, men who are Harley-riding, beer can-crushing, catfish-frying, pool-playing rebels who carry pocketknives instead of pocket combs, go to barbers instead of stylists, wear flannel instead of linen, prefer country-western music to opera, and our executive director has even had a letter printed in *Playboy*.

And yet even though each one of us men here at NAGD is masculine enough to make two average men (and three Frenchmen), we support the contention that Real Men can be both mannered and masculine, can possess both etiquette and a complete set of Phillips screwdrivers.

Through the years we men have been told that Real Men do this and Real Men don't do that. For example, that Real Men do hunt and fish, that Real Men do swear and sweat. That Real Men don't eat quiche, that Real Men don't cry, express their innermost feelings or attend Judy Garland film festivals.

But we here at NAGD contend that whatever it is that Real Men do and don't do, they do it politely. Moreover, a Real Man never feels threatened by manners, never feels that being polite somehow makes him less masculine. Masculinity is a trait, not a trapping. It is not put on and taken off, like articles of clothing. Think about it: John Wayne wearing a leather vest and chaps or wearing a dress and pantyhose would still be John Wayne. True, if you were in a saloon when John Wayne came in wearing a dress and pantyhose, you might not know whether to break a bar stool over his head or flirt with him, but he would still be the same person. A man either has masculinity or he does not. If he does not have it, no amount of tattoos, fights, swagger, bullying or rudeness can achieve it. And if he does have it, no amount of sensitivity or etiquette can remove it.

Please proceed to Chapter 2. "The Duke" would want you to.

2

THE WORM TURNS

Man has come under much scrutiny of late. He has been discussed on talk shows. He has been written about in books. He has been the subject of college courses (three examples: Understanding Man, Accepting Man, Kicking Man in the Shin When He Acts Like a Jerk).

Question: That third course sounds interesting. Are there any prerequisites?

Answer: Yes—six hours of psychology and a pair of high heels with pointed toes.

For generations, our culture's definition of a Real Man was largely unchanged. Real Men were lumberjacks, line-backers, long-haul truckers, cowboys, Mounties, Tarzan,

Bogart and G.I. Joe. Masculinity was measured in terms such as chest and facial hair, tattoos, aggressive behavior and notches on gun barrel and bed post. Real Men were strong and silent. Real Men were tall and strapping. Bigger was better.

But now that definition is changing. The traits that for so long characterized a Real Man are being challenged. Stereotypes of him and by him are being shattered. His life is becoming incredibly complex and competitive. He has come to measure success in nervous tics and pints of stomach acid. Stress is everywhere. A man can't go outside these days without tripping over some stress. "Who left this stress lying in the yard?!" he screams, popping a Tums.

Change is all around him. Communism has failed, the Cold War has ended. Men are wearing ponytails and earrings, women are wearing suits and carrying briefcases. Female reporters have conquered the frontier of men's team locker rooms. Men have had to adjust to the extinction of the muscle car (RIP, GTO), the colorization of *Casablanca*, the approaching retirement of Nolan Ryan, the relocation of the St. Louis Cardinals (and London Bridge) to Arizona and watching actors other than Sean Connery portray James Bond.

Perhaps more importantly, men's relationship with women has been detoured into downtown Upheaval. We now live in a world where anything that a man can do a woman can do and while retaining water. Traditional gender roles are blurring. Women ask men out. Women bring men flowers. Women are the aggressors romantically and sexually. Men date men. Women date women. Men date women who date men who used to be women. Women date men who date women who used to be men. Men date women who date men who used to be women who can whip anyone in this paragraph.

We here at NAGD applaud life's rich diversity, but lately sometimes we get so confused that we envy the lowly earthworm. Each and every earthworm, being hermaphroditic, has both masculine and feminine genders. Not only is this a simpler arrangement, but it also doubles the earthworm's chances of getting a date to the prom.

We here at NAGD trace much of this change back to the 1970s. Something happened in the '70s. Well, actually, a lot happened in the '70s: the Women's Movement, the Sexual Revolution, Hippies, Vietnam, Watergate. Millions of Baby Boomers began to reach an awkward age—too old for diapers, too young for Depends.

In the '70s along came Alan Alda. And Phil Donahue. Suddenly a man was expected to be sensitive, sharing and caring. A man was expected to try to get in touch with his feminine side. We here at NAGD suspect that so far the earthworm has been more successful.

All of this change can leave a man wondering where he stands. How is a Real Man defined today, what is this Real Man's proper niche in society? What is proper male etiquette as the world goes roller-blading and faxing and NordicTracking into the twenty-first century? And when an earthworm dances with itself at the prom, who leads?

The Worm Turns

3

WELL-BRED OR EVINRUDE?

On the surface, etiquette may appear to be more nicety than necessity. Etiquette may seem like just the icing on the cake of culture, just the boutonniere on the lapel of social interaction. Or, to use a metaphor closer to a Real Man's heart, etiquette may seem like just the compression ring on the piston in the outboard motor of the bass boat of life.

Question: Huh?

Answer: Never mind.

But etiquette is much more than nicety. Etiquette makes life livable. Etiquette makes trying times less trying. Etiquette makes an office staff meeting or a blind date less likely to end in an exchange of small-arms fire.

The purpose of etiquette is to make other people feel comfortable and respected and appreciated in a social situation (We here at NAGD define a social situation as any interaction between two or more people, or between two people and an inflatable party doll.).

In essence, etiquette is just another word for the Golden Rule. When we are polite to others, we are extending to them the same rights and privileges that we want for ourselves. Etiquette is remembering that others value their time and space as much as we value ours, that our convenience should never become someone else's inconvenience. Etiquette is remembering that in any social situation, eventually the tables turn. For example, if we double-park our car for our own convenience, inconveniencing other drivers, we should remember that on a later occasion it may be we who are inconvenienced by a double-parker. How will we like it when the Isuzu is on the other foot?

Etiquette is paying attention to details as those details affect other people. And what is life but an endless parade of details? We are born, we tend to details, we die. Then someone else gets to tend to details, such as feeding the thirty-seven cats we leave behind.

But etiquette is much more than tending to the more-obvious details such as always saying "please" and "thank you." Oh, much, much more. The man who coos "please" and "thank you" at every opportunity can still be Randy Rude. Likewise, etiquette is much more than just table manners. The man who at an elegant dinner never uses the wrong fork or never chews with his mouth open can still be an ill-mannered man.

"No man is an island," wrote John Donne, who we here at NAGD contend was a Real Man even though he was (1) a poet and (2) British.

And Donne was right—as individuals we do not live in our own personal vacuums. What we do in our daily life affects others. Far more than we might want to admit. Because admitting that what we do affects others—whether at the dinner table or in the supermarket or on the freeway—

brings with it grave personal responsibility. By our treatment of others (etiquette) we have the power to set bad examples, to irritate, to offend, to inconvenience. Personally, when we here at NAGD think about this grave responsibility, we want to just hole up in our well-equipped home workshop and not come out again until either (1) we're so old that we're actually expected to be rude or (2) we finally finish building that bookcase we've been working on, whichever comes first.

Question: Is a Real Man today ever too busy for etiquette?

Answer: No. Never. Any man who can find time to watch three football games on TV on Thanksgiving Day can also find the time to be considerate of others. Look at Japanese men. They are among the busiest, most industrious and productive men on Earth. Thanks to them, from the air Japan looks like an anthill with bathhouses.

Japanese men work long hours under great stress, get up at 5:00 a.m. each day to have their coronary during breakfast so that they don't have to have it on company time. And yet they are never too busy to be excruciatingly polite. If, for example, their coronary causes them to pitch face forward into someone else's breakfast cereal, they are never too busy to spell out "pardon me" with the corn flakes. If they get stomped on by Godzilla, they are never too busy to apologize to the big guy for getting underfoot. Or if the president of the United States goes to Japan to ask them to buy more American-made cars and suddenly throws up on them, they are never too busy to make America feel less embarrassed by coming to the United States to suddenly throw up on a Chevy.

Similarly, the American Real Man should never be too busy or too preoccupied to be considerate of others. Personally, we here at NAGD contend that if each person were only ten percent more considerate of others, life on this tired old

Excruciatingly Polite

planet would be ninety percent better. That's a bargain at today's prices.

Etiquette is all that separates Real Men from the so-called lower animals. Well, etiquette and a willingness to watch eight straight hours of "Charlie's Angels" reruns.

Question: Have you seen the episode where Sabrina is taken hostage and tied in a chair, and the ropes are real, real tight?

Answer: Yes. Twice.

Question: Does etiquette mean that a Real Man has to like everyone?

Answer: No. And aren't you glad? If the good Lord had wanted us to like everyone, he would not have invented George Steinbrenner.

Etiquette merely means that in every social situation a Real Man should extend certain basic courtesies to everyone, regardless of race, creed or credit card ceiling. Heaven knows we here at NAGD certainly don't like everyone. But we do try to treat everyone as if we do like them. We would treat George Steinbrenner with the same politeness with which we would treat Mother Teresa. Why? Because he is a fellow human being. Until the courts rule otherwise.

We would afford George the same basic minimum courtesies that we would afford anyone else even if he bought Mother Teresa's contract and traded her to Cleveland for two relief pitchers and a missionary to be named later.

Question: Even if Cleveland then sent Mother Teresa down to the minors, where all she got to do was bless the team bus and catch batting practice?

Answer: Yes, and thank you so much for asking.

Mother Teresa at the Plate

4

DR. JEKYLL UNDER
HIS HIDE

Let's take a closer look at this wacky guy we call man. What do we know about him? Well, we know that he's a casual kind of fellow. Typically, he wears his pants so low that when he turns his back to you and bends over, on a clear day you can see forever. His body is capable of producing an assortment of sounds that can cause a whale hundreds of miles out at sea to perk up its ears and ask, "Mommy?"

His wife or girlfriend has had to adjust to having to send canaries in before entering any bathroom he has occupied recently. Just as she has had to accept the fact that he doesn't like to dance and, when coerced to, moves around the floor as if he were wearing snowshoes.

(The man so-described is, of course, a composite. In all

probability there exists no one man who harbors all these characteristics. But if he does exist, rest assured that your daughter will marry him.)

So why all these rough edges on us men? Because for thousands upon thousands of years man was an earthy, outdoorsy hunter, a primitive savage. As humans evolved and moved down from the trees and into caves, man stayed outside in the elements to hunt and to protect. Also to invent the wheel and to discover fire—two developments in human history whose importance can scarcely be overestimated. After all, because of the wheel and fire today we have rolling barbecue grills.

Only in the past few hundreds of years (and especially in the past twenty-five) has man been expected to be anything but rough and uncouth. But now he is expected to be a highly evolved, highly intelligent, highly sensitive thinker. He is under pressure to make a smooth and quick transition from the club and spear to the briefcase and cellular phone. He has had to redirect his courage from facing a wild beast to facing his boss, whom he perceives as having as much power as God but a larger office.

In a way, the changes that man has undergone since his beginnings have been largely superficial. If man's total time on Earth were represented by an onion, the twentieth century would be the thin skin on the outside of the onion. His primitive past would be all those inner rings—the core of the onion. And if you bite an onion, do you taste the skin or the core?

Question: We don't care for onions. Could you restate this analogy using, for example, apples, celery, walnuts or mayonnaise?

Answer: Yes, we could, but *we* don't care for Waldorf salad.

Man's thousands of years as a primitive hunter and man's relatively few years as a soft and civilized city-dweller create a tension within him.

Because of man's primitive past and civilized present, he can comfortably accommodate within the same body seemingly contradictory values and feelings.

Man in his primitive mode has given the world most of its wars and bar fights, committed most of the crime, belched, scratched, spit, worn Nehru jackets and gold medallions, invented dwarf-tossing, buffalo hunts and the appellation "little lady."

But man in his civilized mode also has given the world immortal works of art, literature, poetry and music.

Capable of the loftiest charity and the lowest depravity, man is Gandhi and Genghis Khan, St. Francis of Assisi and Attila the Hun. He is Pat Boone and Daniel Boone, Gary Cooper and Alice Cooper. Scratch Fred Rogers, and you'll find Fred Flintstone. Scratch Al Schweitzer, and you'll find Al Bundy.

Question: How could all these men be members of the same gender?

Answer: Heck, all these men could be members of the same bowling team.

Question: So is a Real Man a primitive savage or a sensitive gentleman?

Answer: Yes, and thank you so much for asking.

5

GOON WITH THE WIND

This duality explains why man acts as he does, why he can be suave one moment and uncouth the next. He has one foot in the cave and one foot in the board room. He is an ape in wing-tips, a Neanderthal with a fax machine. Oh, he may dress in tie and tails, but underneath there remains the primitive, uncouth savage just waiting to burst out. Probably during his wife's formal dinner party.

Question: What is the most uncouth, uncivilized throwback to man's primitive beginnings?

Answer: Many women would probably reply: "my ex-husband."

Close, but no alimony. The correct answer is: the belch.

Prim-itive and Proper

In the beginning, God created man from the dust of the ground and breathed air into him. Man has been letting that air leak back out ever since.

Today the belch might well stand as a metaphor for man's primitive nature. Granted, it's not a very pretty metaphor. It's no "The moon was a ghostly galleon tossed upon cloudy seas," but, hey, we're talking stomach gas here, not celestial whitecaps.

Much as they may try not to, most men belch now and then. Certainly we here at NAGD do on occasion. Why, the president of the United States of America belches, when his busy schedule allows. The difference is that when the president of the United States of America belches, Peter Jennings breaks in on "General Hospital" with a bulletin, Miss Manners is asked to provide her expert analysis, and Saddam Hussein interprets the entire incident as an anti-Arab gesture.

So let's face it: Men belch. But today's Real Men belch downwind (Are you taking notes, Earl?). A Real Man is aware of his primitive side and tries to spare others its full force. If he feels a belch about to blossom, he takes steps to minimize or divert what the sixteenth-century writer called its "corrupt fumosytye." After all, people around him don't want to be reminded that just beyond a Real Man's strikingly handsome smile, digestive processes are breaking down a Big Mac into the very building blocks of life: proteins, carbohydrates and gristle.

Question: What are, oh, eleven things that a woman would rather hear her man do than belch?

Answer: Glad you asked. They include: suck his teeth, gargle, snore, sing a medley of Slim Whitman songs, recite obscure sports statistics, talk in his sleep, speak in tongues, take up for Mike Tyson, yodel, wolf whistle at her sister, wolf whistle at her brother.

More No-Nose

And then there's man's endearing habit of picking his nose with his finger: a colorful peccadillo that began millions of years ago, shortly after man evolved (1) a nose and (2) a finger. But the habit really began to flourish after 1912, when a man named Lester Farnsworth Wire of Salt Lake City invented the traffic signal. Suddenly, red lights gave men a municipally decreed time-out in their schedule during which they could pick their nose, thus freeing up the rest of their busy day to devote to more significant endeavors, namely digging wax out of their ear canals with a car key.

Nose-picking shows the duality of man: The same finger that can coax music from a piano or hold a scalpel during life-saving surgery, the most dexterous of body parts, the organ of touch and grasp, this lofty digit, this Renaissance pinkie—which in groups of five builds cathedrals, writes sonnets, paints masterpieces and carves sculptures—during red lights can be found loitering in the male nose. This is not unlike finding Michelangelo loitering in a Dumpster.

Question: Does a man who picks his nose at red lights think that no one else can see him or what?

Answer: Apparently he does. He thinks that being inside his car renders him invisible to those around him, thus allowing him to pick his nose in complete privacy. Meanwhile, people in other cars are looking at him in disgust, and Gray Line sightseeing buses are pulling alongside him and pausing so that tourists from out of town can gawk at him and snap photos.

In addition, at any given time, high in the sky, military reconnaissance satellites are transmitting back to Earth global images of thousands of men picking their nose at red lights. Sometimes members of the Pentagon sit and watch the satellite monitors, pointing and chuckling far into the night.

We here at NAGD suspect that this is why more and more women are giving men gift certificates to get their car windows tinted.

The nose has another use, of course: It is used to sneeze with. Sure, Real Men sneeze. But Real Men sneeze as quietly as is medically recommendable, being mindful afterward to apologize to others for any important papers scattered, livestock stampeded or furniture blown over. Not that we here at NAGD are suggesting that a Real Man sneeze as many women do: by sealing off nose and mouth and daintily trying to contain the force of the eruption in a barely audible "eek." Each year hundreds of women explode while trying to contain a sneeze. Typically, makeup, earrings, jewelry, girdles, purse, skirt and blouse are scattered over several city blocks. The vice president of the United States hovers over the scene in a helicopter, tsk-tsks and declares the area a disaster area qualified for federal aid and a big box of Kleenex.

Spit Happens

Sure, a Real Man feels the need to spit from time to time. But he remembers this simple fact: The animal best known for spitting is the camel. Camels also chew their cud, have knobby knees and breath that can defoliate a small forest. A Real Man would not want to have anything in common with any animal that with a single sigh can put Chip and Dale among the homeless.

To Itch Is Human, To Scratch Divine

Spitting often is accompanied by scratching. The two habits seem to be paired together, like fire and brimstone, or assault and battery, or Regis and Kathie Lee. We here at NAGD suspect that scratching among men has been encouraged by the proliferation of baseball games on TV. After all, a man watching a baseball game sees superstars scratching themselves before a TV audience of millions, often scratching areas of the body that would be described, in strike-zone terms, as low and inside. Ryne Sandberg, Roger Clemens, Darryl Strawberry, Don Mattingly, Mookie Wilson: The list is almost endless. When a man watches such behavior, it reinforces and influences. Mookie see, Mookie do.

A man watches talented, idolized and heavily jewelryed superstars scratching themselves in public and says defensively to his wife: "Look: *Those* guys scratch themselves. And *they* earn $3 million a year."

To which his wife replies: "Yeah, but a $3 million salary means those guys get approximately $734 per scratch. If *you* can get $734 per scratch, I'll dump an ant farm down your pants."

Etiquette aside, scratching on the baseball field can be confusing to the players. When a base coach inadvertently mixes his groin scratches and fanny digs with his signals to a runner, the runner doesn't know whether the coach is instructing him to (1) steal second or (2) meet the coach after the game for sushi and slow dancing.

Anyway, no one wants to watch you scratch yourself. If you must scratch, excuse yourself. Do it in private. In public, don't try to scratch yourself by disguising the act, such as by announcing at lunch, "Pshaw. I seem to have dropped a slice of roast beef down my pants. How clumsy of me. I'll just take my fork and reach down here and ahhhhhhhhhhhhhhhhhhhhhhhhhhh."

Likewise, do not try to sneak in a scratch while creating a diversion: "Hey, look over there! Isn't that Queen Elizabeth kissing a yak? Ahhhhhhhhhhhhhhhhhhhhhhhhhhhhh."

Where's the Fork?

The Mother of Intention

Let's face it—certainly we men know better than to belch and scratch and spit, etc. Most of us men were taught by our mothers since we were knee-high to a Nehi that it is impolite to belch and scratch and spit, etc. Which may explain why we belch and scratch and spit, etc. *Because Mother told us not to.* Disobeying Mother is a major tenet in the Guy Laws. As proof, look at the other motherly maxims that we ignored:

"Don't smoke—it will stunt your growth."

"Don't cross your eyes—they might get stuck that way."

"Don't go swimming immediately after a meal—you'll get cramps and drown."

"Don't pet stray animals—you don't know where they've been."

All of you doubting Thomases have to concede the validity of these four maxims every time you see a short, cross-eyed dead man with fleas.

Similarly, when Mother told us that self-abuse leads to blindness, we again scoffed and ignored her. Which you men know if you're reading the Braille edition of this book.

But perhaps the most common admonition from Mother through the ages has been: "Don't play with sharp, pointed objects because" (All together now, men, shout it loud, shout it proud!) *"You'll put somebody's eye out."*

As far as we could tell, Mother defined "sharp, pointed objects" as "anything you want to play with"—sticks, slingshots, BB guns, toads. But we here at NAGD would point out that the human race has actually benefited infinitely because, now and then, boys have disobeyed that particular admonition from Mother. Think about it: If little Willie Shakespeare had heeded his mother and never picked up that sharp, pointed quill, the world today might not have *Macbeth* and *Othello*. If little Tommy Edison and little Alex Bell had never picked up the sharp, pointed tools of the inventor, today the world might not have electric lights and the telephone. We'd all be sitting around in the dark wondering why no one ever calls us.

Question: In addition to belching, don't men produce another form of gas that most women won't even say the word for, much less do?

Answer: Yes. In an ideal world, only anesthesiologists would pass gas. But this is not an ideal world. If it were, Walt Disney would never have let Old Yeller get rabies.

What with a man's belching and flatulence, at times he must seem to a woman like a veritable Mount St. Helen's of bodily eruptions. A municipal gas company with five-o'clock shadow. A woman might well wonder how the same gender that gave the world the sounds of Beethoven's *fifth Symphony* and Handel's *Messiah* can also give the world sounds that even a walrus would find unbecoming. Thus the lament of Mrs. Earl is typical. We here at NAGD keep a running list of the phrases that women have used to describe the sounds that their man's body is capable of.

Question: What are, oh, eleven of those phrases?

Answer: Glad you asked. They include: a chair leg scraping on a wooden floor, a deflating balloon flying around a room, a foghorn, a thunder clap, a Bronx cheer, a tuba in pain, a bagpipe in heat, a hog, a bull-frog, a duck, a duck going through a duck press.

Of course, no one, not even a Real Man, can will his body to not produce gas. He can control his checkbook, his crab-grass and his cholesterol, but not his own intestinal processes. From time to time, his eruptions defy him, embarrass him, betray him. Most often in a crowded elevator.

But, as when he belches, a Real Man tries to prevent, delay, or at least minimize his intestinal outbursts. And at home, when a Real Man commits such a faux pas, he definitely does not blame it on his dog. Especially if his dog is at the vet's at the time. (The phrase "faux pas" is, in fact, French for "le dog did it.")

Question: What are eight things that a man's dog would

rather be falsely accused of than passing his master's gas?

Answer: Chewing the furniture, digging up the geraniums, staining the carpet, biting the mailman, chasing a hearse, cheating on finals in obedience school, giving rabies to Old Yeller, checking into a cheap Washington, D.C., motel room with Socks.

Question: Does Phil Donahue ever emit gas?

Answer: No. In fact—and not many people know this—Phil Donahue has no body orifices. When he reaches age seventy or so it is expected that he will simply explode.

Question: Might we see a chronology that shows low points in the history of masculine etiquette?

Answer: Yes, and thank you so much for asking.

400 million B.C.: The human race's earliest primordial ancestors (two single-celled organisms) evolve sufficiently to slither ashore from the sea; the female works hard to establish a tidy, cozy home in a tide pool, the male sits down on the beach to wait for the bikini to evolve.

2 million B.C.: The human race descends from the apes and moves down out of the trees; the apes tell the women to write often, the apes tell the men that they will not get their cleaning deposit back.

500,000 B.C.: Primitive men engage in the first belching contest.

499,999 B.C.: Primitive women consider moving back up into the trees.

3,600 B.C.: An able-bodied Mesopotamian man invents the wheel.

3,599 B.C.: An able-bodied Mesopotamian man parks in a handicapped space.

218 B.C.: Traveling from Spain to Italy, Hannibal breaks wind while crossing the Alps, blames it on one of his elephants.

217 B.C.: The elephants get even with Hannibal by leading his army in the wrong direction.

216 B.C.: Hannibal reaches the outskirts of Topeka.

1215 A.D.: In England the Magna Carta is drawn up, granting the common man certain inalienable rights, among them the right to expectorate in public.

1216 A.D.: The Magna Carta is taken off public display after it is found to have saliva stains on it.

1501 A.D.: As the Renaissance flourishes in Europe with a resurgence in arts and science, after months of visionary thinking, Leonardo da Vinci completes initial blueprints for an improved obscene gesture.

1845 A.D.: Robert Browning receives a poignant and heartfelt love letter from Elizabeth Barrett, sends it back to her with the grammar corrected.

1912 A.D.: The traffic signal is invented.

1913 A.D.: The first instance of gridlock is recorded as twenty-seven male drivers idle at a traffic signal picking their nose.

1954 A.D.: Howard Stern is born.

6

MISTER AND MYTHS

OK, enough about belching and scratching. This is the chapter that many of you paid your $6.95 for: the man-and-woman stuff. Without further ado, let's gird our loins and open up this can of worms to see who goes to the prom.

Men traditionally have been somewhat in awe of women. To men, women are strange, fascinating, enigmatic creatures. Riddles wrapped in mysteries wrapped in silk blouses. After all, to a man a woman has special powers: She can understand a cookbook, she can thread a needle, she can make a living, breathing baby person using just a few pounds of protoplasm and a faulty diaphragm.

Question: Wait a minute. Let's give man his due. Doesn't he contribute to the miracle of birth?

Answer: Certainly he does—he assembles the crib.

Thus for hundreds of years men bestowed upon women social deferences. A man brought a woman flowers and candy. He lit her cigarette, opened doors for her, helped her on with her coat, walked at curbside beside her to protect her from mud splashed from the road and from chamber pots emptied from windows above. In restaurants he pulled out chairs for her, ordered for her. He always picked up the check. On sinking ships, his lifeboat protocol was women and children first. For centuries, he carried her books to school, later got down onto one knee to propose to her, still later picked her up and carried her over the threshold. No wonder he walks the way he does.

In short, traditionally man put woman on a pedestal. "Sure, he did," the cynical woman of today scoffs, "so that he could look up her dress."

Nonetheless, for our fathers and grandfathers etiquette toward women was a simple, fairly clear-cut matter. Customs had been in place for centuries. But now that attitudes of and about women are changing, how does a Real Man know how to treat women with the etiquette they prefer? Frankly, this one is a toughie. We here at NAGD try to analyze the issue and soon have to go into a darkened room and lie down with a cool, damp cloth over our face.

What are the rules today? As far as we here at NAGD can tell, the number one rule is: There is no rule. At least not like there once was. We here at NAGD have interviewed many women about how they want to be treated by a man, and we can find no real consensus. We asked our mother and sister, our girlfriend, our wife, our ex-wife and our ex-wife's female divorce lawyer. Our wife gave us one answer, our ex-wife gave us another, and our ex-wife's female divorce lawyer gave us a restraining order.

How a Real Man should treat a woman is a complex, ever-evolving, many-sided, emotionally charged issue. For generations most women wanted to be called "Miss" or "Mrs." Now some want to be called "Ms." For generations most women wanted to be treated like "ladies." Now some want to be treated like "women." Either way is fine with a Real Man, but the trick is knowing which woman prefers which treatment. Were Sir Walter Raleigh to spread his coat over a mud puddle for three different women today, the first woman might think him gracious, the second woman might think him insulting, the third woman might call a cop because some weirdo wearing a doublet, pantaloons and ruffled collar is waving his coat over some mud while saying "forsooth" a lot.

Same with opening doors for women. Some women regard having a door opened for them as offensive—a relic of the chauvinistic past. But some women still regard having a door opened for them by men as genteel. Ditto all the other heretofore-polite gestures of man toward woman. How is the Real Man to know? Of course, a Real Man might consider actually asking the woman her preferences, but we here at NAGD realize that that would be coming perilously close to communication—something for which men have not been famous.

So, for those men who can't "read" a woman, who don't trust their instincts or masculine intuition, here is a form to give to the woman—whether she is a date, a friend, a colleague or a stranger:

Etiquette Form

Real Man etiquette means treating people with respect, but respect means different things to different people. So please answer these questions so that I can avoid offending you or creating an awkward situation for us both:

My feelings about a man...

1.	opening doors for me	like	dislike	no opinion
2.	standing when I enter a room	like	dislike	no opinion
3.	ordering for me at a restaurant	like	dislike	no opinion
4.	helping me on with my coat	like	dislike	no opinion
5.	pulling my chair out for me	like	dislike	no opinion
6.	calling me "Miss" or "Mrs."	like	dislike	no opinion
7.	lighting my cigarette	like	dislike	trying to quit

On a date, I feel it is acceptable for a woman to...

8. pick up the man in her car   yes   no   no opinion
9. pick up the check for dinner   yes   no   no opinion
10. give the man a good-night kiss   yes   no   no opinion
11. give the man a good-night condom   yes   no   no opinion

Essay question: I would like to see Andrew Dice Clay in a lot of pain because:

_____

_____

_____

_____

_____

_____

_____

This brings us to the male libido. It is legendary. Mythical. It is the stuff that dreams (and the topless bar industry) are made of. And we all can blame it on testosterone. A Real Man who weighs, say, two hundred pounds is fifty pounds of flesh, fifty pounds of bone, ten pounds of belt buckle and ninety pounds of testosterone. Testosterone is the hormone that fuels a man's libido and triggers his masculine characteristics, such as growth of facial hair, a deep voice and the tendency, when no one else is around, to stare at himself in a mirror, cock an eyebrow, flare a nostril, flex his muscles and growl, "That's right, Baby. Beg for it."

But even though a Real Man celebrates the difference between the sexes, he tries not to let that difference rule his life. He keeps in mind the fact that regardless of how soft yet firm women are or how sweet they smell or how sultry their smile is or how long their legs are or how good they look wearing only spiked heels and a roll of Saran....Sorry. We here at NAGD seem to have gotten a bit lost in our thoughts. As we started to say, a Real Man keeps in mind the fact that

Flaring and Flexing

women are people first and women second. We here at NAGD have noticed that women are better at keeping this in mind than we men are.

A Real Man has learned that sometimes he has to sublimate his sexual urges. Traditionally, this sublimation has taken diverse and subtle forms. Man has channeled it into sports, hobbies, art, literature, music, architecture. For example, the architect who designed the Leaning Tower of Pisa obviously was sublimating a fantasy about a tall Mediterranean woman with a limp.

And yet considering how much time the average man spends thinking about sex, he knows more about the Chevy fuel system than he does about a woman's reproductive system. This is partly because the Chevy fuel system is very similar to a man's own reproductive system—forty-eight inches of copper tubing, a few valves and a carburetor-like organ located near his spleen. This explains why during sex a man often screams, "Vapor lock! Vapor lock!"

Question: How does a Real Man feel about sexual harassment?

Answer: Sexual harassment is, of course, totally unacceptable to a Real Man. Whenever a Real Man has any doubts about the propriety of something that he is considering saying or doing to a woman, he should picture the woman as a man. Ideally, Ernest Borgnine. Would the Real Man still say it/do it to Ernest Borgnine?

We here at NAGD admit that men have at times been heels to women through the years. But we men also have been fed some pretty bad advice about how to treat women. Here is some actual advice—included in a pamphlet titled *How to Make Love* written by Hugh Morris in 1936—to young men on how to persist in achieving that all-important first kiss with a young woman:

"If she flinches, don't worry. If she flinches and makes an outcry, don't worry. If she flinches, makes an outcry and tries to get up from the sofa, don't worry....However, if she flinches, makes an outcry, a loud, stentorian outcry, mind you, and starts to scratch your face, then start to worry..."

Whew. We here at NAGD were beginning to wonder if ol' Hugh would *ever* start to worry. Needless to say, a young man who attempted to press his advantage so unchivalrously upon today's young woman would never again be able to pucker without the aid of a trained chimp.

Buoys and Gulls

Another complaint that we here at NAGD hear from women is that their men spend too much time away from them indulging in Guy Stuff— such as fishing. Again the key is compromise. A Real Man gives equal time to his woman's interests. Let's say that a group of men suddenly come into a generous sum of money, and, using creative bookkeeping, use that money to buy a fully rigged bass boat that they had been dreaming of for months. Let's say further that those men bear no resemblance to any of us here at NAGD. Nosiree. These men who bought the fully rigged bass boat are imaginary. And live in another state. And are much taller than we are. Anyway, ideally if these men take their bass boat out on Saturday, they should then do something of their wives' choosing on Sunday. If, for example, one of the wives wants to go to a ballet, her husband should willingly go with her.

The Call of the Mild

Or better yet, why not ask your wife to join you in Guy Stuff? Such as camping. After all, women have at last broken the glass ceiling. Why not the canvas ceiling? But before you go camping with your wife, do keep in mind that women may perceive the outdoors differently than men do, seeing it basically as a handy place to keep lawns, clouds and the meter reader. Women see the outdoors as being made up largely of nature, which they perceive as most often manifesting itself in the form of (1) dirt and (2) insects.

Keep in mind that a woman may have different standards for camping. For example, she may not agree with you that the other side of a tree qualifies as a rest room. So pitch camp near toilet facilities that she finds acceptable. She may not share your cave man fascination with staring into a smoky, swirling campfire. She may not even share the joy of sleeping on cold, hard ground, eating gritty food and swatting mosquitoes large enough to be detected on radar.

So it's up to you to show her how much fun camping can be. Get her involved in the various camping activities— pitching the tent, unrolling the sleeping bags, building the campfire, gathering the wood, jumping into the lake after she is attacked by a nest of hornets.

And Don't Forget St. Patrick Ewing's Day

We men are notorious for not remembering dates that are special to women—wedding anniversary, their birthday, Mother's Day, Valentine's Day. And yet your wife might well argue that any man who can remember Lou Gehrig's batting average for 1934, Joe Namath's pass-completion percentage for 1969 and Wilt Chamberlain's high-point game for 1966 can also remember your wedding anniversary, if only because that was also the date that Rocky Marciano knocked out Joe Walcott in 1952.

To remember dates that are important to a woman, a Real Man should try this simple associative memory trick. Let's say that your wedding anniversary is December 15. Think D 15. D as in Dickerson. And how many touchdowns did Eric Dickerson rush for in 1983? You know that—15. Or if your wife's birthday is September 24, think S 24. How can you remember that? Simple—S as in Stephens. In 1945 Vern Stephens of St. Louis won the American League home run title with how many? Easy—24.

(Note of caution: If this associative memory trick helps you to remember your wife's birthday, no good will come of it if you then forgetfully give her a locket that has engraved on it: "Happy birthday to my precious wife Vern.")

Present Imperfect

Giving gifts to women—as on anniversaries, birthdays, Christmas—traditionally has been a nicety where we men have shown little imagination and taste. The male spider who brings his female spider a fly shows more imagination and taste. We men usually resort to buying the woman (1) a bottle of cheap perfume or (2) an article of gaudy clothing.

The fate of such bad gifts is inevitable—the recipient is too polite to reveal her true feelings, even feigns delight, much as the female spider does with the gift fly ("How lovely! And its legs are still twitching!"). Then, when you aren't looking, the woman chunks these bottles of cheap perfume and articles of gaudy clothing onto a closet shelf, where they pile up over the years. Tragically, eventually one day she goes to that closet after an anniversary or birthday or Christmas, opens the door, and the bottles of perfume and articles of clothing come crashing down on her. In the local newspaper the headline reads: "Woman, 34, fatally Shalimared."

Next time, ask a trusted female friend if she thinks your woman would like a nice fly.

Even then, you'll probably buy the wrong size.

Woman, 34, Fatally Shalimared

Beauty Is in the (Black) Eye of the Beholder

A Real Man does not ogle other women while he is in the company of the woman who wishes that he'd ogle *her* once in a while. When you are at the beach with your wife, don't gawk at thong-clad nymphettes. When watching "The Today Show" with your girlfriend, don't talk dirty to Katie Couric. Don't leaf through your wife's *Victoria's Secret* catalogue while saying, "I'd like to have *this* one and *this* one and *this* one" unless you're referring to the black lace teddys.

Dating Do's and Dunce

Dating is a time-honored form of social interaction, but today it is more complicated than ever for a Real Man. It calls for increased sensitivity and adaptability. A Real Man needs to have the insight of Freud, the wisdom of Solomon, the sexual knowledge of Kinsey, the diplomacy of Kissinger and the flexibility of Gumby.

Question: Whatever became of Gumby, anyway?

Answer: Gumby is semi-retired now, works as a crossing guard at an arts-and-crafts school.

When on a date, remember that conversation is a dialogue, not a monologue. Remember that a Real Man—although also primitive—is a sharing, caring creature. Ideally, he talks "with," not "to," a woman. Just as ideally he makes love "with," not "to," a woman. "With" is a bilateral preposition, "to" is a unilateral preposition.

When you talk with the woman, it's polite to make eye contact. Look her squarely in the eyes. If you are too shy, fake it—look her squarely in the nose. But remember that at close range, this can cause your own eyes to cross, and they might get stuck that way, and then your mother would bend over your hospital bed and crow, "I told you so," and you'd want to throw a bed pan at both of her.

On a date a Real Man also does not try to control the evening. Any man who likes to go Dutch treat should be willing to split other aspects of the date. Do not dictate every detail of what the two of you do—where you eat, which movie you see, where you sit at the restaurant and the theater. Ask the woman her preferences. Compromise. If, for example, she wants to go to the circus, but you want to see a Clint Eastwood movie, do both. First go to the circus. If she runs away with the lion-tamer (After all, he *is* brave, rugged and owns his own whip.), be philosophical: At least at the movie you won't have to share your popcorn.

Sometimes disagreements occur when a man and a woman are in public. But a Real Man never causes a scene. Remember that people around you are embarrassed to have to witness something that should be a private exchange between two people. Don't argue conspicuously, no matter what. No doubt you yourself have had to witness the thinly veiled angry exchanges between couples in public. All is calm, then suddenly the man and woman at the table next to you are Mr. Serb and Miss Croat. They raise their voices, silverware is rattled. You try not to look or listen. Their exchange becomes more vocal. United Nations peacekeep-

Public Display of Aggression

ing troops are air-dropped over the couple's table. You and other diners within earshot begin sinking down in your seats in embarrassment. Lower and lower. Soon your eyes are level with the table top. Unless peace is restored, you may actually eat your dessert *under* the table.

And, by the same token, don't subject people to embarrassing public displays of affection. For example, do not kiss in a theater line. Do not embrace passionately during high Mass. Do not consummate your marriage on public transportation.

Beaus and Arrows

If you have a date with a woman who has children, extend the same courtesies to the child that you extend to the parent. Be polite. Don't condescend. Remember that kids are people, too, only built closer to the ground. Include the child in activities and conversations. For example, if your date and you are trying to have a quiet evening at her place, but her son keeps running through the house playing with his Little Dickens archery set, sit him on your knee and ask him, "Hey, Billy, why don't you help me think of five ways to get this arrow out of my chest without bleeding on my vest?"

Home Is Where the (Cross Your) Heart Is

Before entertaining a woman in your home, clean up your act. Single men tend to live, shall we say, casually. So before admitting a woman into your home, make an honest and objective assessment of your housekeeping skills. Does your kitchen look like a fungus ranch? If you have a pet, is there enough fur on the sofa to knit another pet? Are there great gray heaps of dirty boxer shorts scattered around the floor? Have these heaps reached underwear critical mass and evolved into primitive life-forms—weird creatures with two short legs and a flap for a mouth?

A Real Man makes the woman feel special. So go through your home getting rid of artifacts of past dates with other women. No woman wants to glance up during a critically intimate moment and see a size thirty-eight bra hanging from the chandelier. Especially if she wears a thirty-two.

Much Adieu about Nothing

At the conclusion of a date, it is natural to want to say something polite to the woman. But don't say to her, "I'll give you a call real soon" or "Let's get together again real soon" if you have no such intention. Such empty, off-handed promises are dating's equivalent of "The check's in the mail."

Be polite, but don't send false signals. The following sign-offs are recommended:

"Thank you for a delightful evening."

"I had a really nice time."

"Well, I guess, I'll just be driving myself to the emergency room now."

If you tell a woman that you will call her, she just might be unreasonable enough to think that you will call her. She might even sit around the house waiting for the phone to ring. Time passes. Autumn comes. Then winter. Then spring. The snow melts. The trees bud. Finally her phone rings. She answers. It's a man's voice! Her heart sings.

The man's voice asks her if she has ever considered the many advantages of aluminum siding.

She rents the film *Thelma and Louise,* and proceeds to watch it thirty-four times.

Here is a form for an after-date thank-you note:

Dear [name]:

I just wanted to drop you a line to thank you for a wonderful/ so-so/hideously unbearable evening. You were quite charming/tolerable/abominable. The conversation was delightful/adequate/asinine, and dinner at the restaurant that you recommended was delicious/palatable/still moving. And afterward, dancing with you has left me dazzled/unmoved/unable to move. I sincerely look forward to talking with you again soon/seeing you again soon/reading your obituary.

Until then, I am
thinking of you,/
thinking of someone else,/
thinking of filing charges,
[signature]

Question: When a couple splits, what is the proper etiquette for the man?

Answer: If the split is her idea, the man should not cry or beg. She feels badly enough as it is. If the split is his idea, he should break it to her gently in a setting that is neutral, private and nonthreatening. This pretty much rules out the hot tub of his new squeeze.

Round Yon Haagen-Dazs

When greeting a woman acquaintance who has gained considerable girth since you last saw her, do *not* ask her when her baby is due unless you are dead-solid *certain* that she is, indeed, pregnant. Do you have proof? For example, have you read a doctor's lab report? Did you personally see the home pregnancy test indicator turn blue? Are you a friend of the late rabbit's family?

We here at NAGD personally know of several men who have committed this social gaffe—assumed that a woman was pregnant and made comments based on this assumption when in truth the woman had merely been hitting the fudge ripple ice cream. These men tell us that their bandages will be removed soon.

Saving Face

A Real Man always tells a woman if she has something on her face that does not belong there—an eyelash on her cheek, a bit of spinach between her teeth, a crumb on her chin. Tell the woman the second you notice. Never put it off —"Oh, by the way, three days ago you had a crumb on your chin the size of another chin." The woman will not appreciate the delay. Especially if the crumb is still there.

Aisles of Smiles

Don't pout when you accompany a woman while she shops. Sure, men and women have different interests and approaches when it comes to shopping. To a man, shopping in department stores or supermarkets is a means to an end. He takes a guerrilla approach—get in, grab item, get out. But to a woman, shopping in a department store or supermarket is likely to be an end in itself—an opportunity to commune with her consumer side, to update her knowledge of the ever-changing retail market, to search for inspiration among the dizzying array of products.

Be patient with her in the department store or supermarket. Remember—the tables always turn. Some day *she* may accompany *you* to the hardware store or to the sporting goods store, and those are *your* weakness. You won't want her to be pouting and hurrying you while you paw almost sensually through the bins of lock washers or the shelves of fishing lures.

The other day Ernie—a research assistant here at NAGD's Department of Etiquette and Hand Tools—took his wife with him to the hardware store. She never tried to hurry him. Not even when he became so entranced while examining some close-out items in the sockets aisle that come closing time he had to be put onto a dolly and wheeled out to their car. His wife had to drive him home while he stared glassy eyed into space and muttered, "Metric hex-head sockets only eighty-nine cents. Metric hex-head sockets only eighty-nine cents."

Ernie's doctor says that he will be fine, but that he shouldn't try to work on any imported cars for two weeks.

Handyman Husband Hexed

7

TO INSURE DOMESTIC TRANQUILITY

Wash and Weary

A Real Man spends much of his time at home with his family—happily communicating with his wife, contentedly sharing quality time with his children, dreamily counting the money in the jar that contains his secret Catch the Next Greyhound Leaving Town, Fake My Own Death, Grow a Beard and Live on the California Coast as a Beachcomber With an Unlisted Dune Fund.

And while he is at home with his family, a Real Man helps with the household chores. This is not always easy. Sometimes he actually hinders more than he helps. When he tries to fold a towel it may look like a final exam in origami class. When he tries to dry a load of clothes his wife's blouses may shrink so much that a Barbie doll would have to let out the darts to fit into them.

But he keeps trying, even though when he does the laundry, he is intimidated by the washing instructions on clothing labels, by the dials on the washing machine, by the temperature settings on the dryer. But he reminds himself that if a Real Man can master a router or a band saw or a fishing rod, he can master a washer and dryer. The trick, he knows, is to read the instructions carefully, be confident and don't make any sudden, uncertain movements. Home appliances can sense fear.

Man has not always helped around the house, of course. Certainly primitive man did not help around the cave. Every time primitive woman would ask primitive man to help clean or cook or help with the kids, he would pretend to be busy. "Can't right now, Honey—I'm evolving." Then, because he knew she was watching him, he'd clench his fists, close his eyes right tight and grimace, as if he were straining to evolve into Dick Cavett by nightfall. In actuality, of course, he was, in his mind's eye, picturing a primitive Greyhound bus.

Homo Sapiens at Home

A Real Man also spends much of his time at work. And when he has had a bad day at work, he doesn't bring it home with him and take it out on his family. After all, if his boss is a jerk, it's the boss he is upset with, not his wife and kids.

Question: We, too, have a boss who is a jerk. Would anyone like to go halvesies on a pie in the face?

Answer: We here at NAGD refuse to condone or abet petty violence. But on weekends you might contact Steve in our Department of Etiquette and Meringue.

TV Guyed

A man's couch is his castle, of course. More so even than his home itself, which the mortgage company owns and merely lets him furnish and paint and repair, etc. On his sofa, a man rules. He can put his feet up on the coffee table, kick back and relax. He is king of the cushions. Lord of all he surveys. Most of all, he is commander in chief of the TV remote control. At the whim of his thumb, Geraldo, Oprah, Montel, Maury, Sally, ad nauseam, come and go: "....So tell my audience, Mr. Dalrymple, when you first realized that in a past life you were a cocker span-" [click] "....Now let me get this straight—every member of our panel today claims to have had sex with at least 1,500 Elvis impersona-" [click] "....Well, Geraldo, then these aliens from the planet Doofus beamed me into their space craft, where they spanked me with a large stalk of aspara-" [click].

But a Real Man is secure enough to let go of the remote control, allowing other members of the household equal time. He keeps in mind the fact that not everyone wants to watch what he wants to watch.

Question: Such as a film version of "Hamlet" performed by the cast of "Gilligan's Island"?

Answer: Yes. We felt that it was a powerful and penetrating interpretation, with Bob Denver never more convincing as the melancholy Dane and Jim Backus perfectly cast as Ophelia.

Question: Speaking of control, what electric blanket set-ting would you recommend that a wife use for a husband who hogs the heat control?

Answer: Turn the heat setting to "CREMATE."

Snips and Snails

All too often a man neglects to trim his toenails. Why? We here at NAGD subscribe to the theory that man is reluctant to trim his toenails because they are vestiges of the claws he had before he evolved into Homo sapien. They are ten sharp reminders of his primitive past when he roamed barefoot and unfettered over the plains and through the forests as a proud and powerful hunter.

Regardless, a Real Man trims his toenails. At least as often as he trims the Christmas tree.

And, ever mindful of the sensitivities (and safety) of family members, he does this alone and in another room. Preferably another room in another state. Preferably another state that no one is using. Montana is usually available.

Smoking Etiquette

See preceding paragraph.

Water Hazard

We here at NAGD receive many inquiries from women regarding that most-vexing shortcoming of the semi-domesticated man: the seeming inability to "hit" the toilet bowl cleanly from a distance that—let's face it, men—if the bathroom were a golf green, would qualify for a gimme.

The sports analogy is not accidental. We here at NAGD think that the solution to this masculine shortcoming is to exploit man's intense interest in sports that require eye-hand coordination. This interest can be traced to man's thousands of years as a hunter—he had to be swift and sure with his spear, throw it far and true. Now that he no longer chases wild animals or chucks spears, he chases golf balls toward a hole or chucks basketballs at a hoop. We here at NAGD have noticed that this preoccupation with trying to propel an object into a round container from a distance finds expression in even the most mundane tasks—throwing dirty clothes into an open hamper, throwing wadded-up pieces of paper into a trash can (Personally, we give ourselves two points for a shirt, three points for a final notice from the collection agency.).

The lesson for a woman here is obvious—to give her man an incentive to hit the toilet bowl, she should turn the process into a game of skill: Hang a basketball net around the rim of the bowl. Hardwood court and peanut vendors optional.

This should do the trick. However, motivating her little shooter to put the seat down after the final buzzer is another challenge altogether.

Child's Play

Sure, a man's child is the strongest, smartest, most-adorable, most-talented child in any sporting event, stage production, recital or school talent show. But a Real Man tries to be humble. During your child's school's Christmas play, don't brag to other parents about what a great "third sheep from the left in the nativity scene" your child is. They won't hear you anyway—they'll be too busy bragging about what a great Second Cow From the Right *their* child is.

At your child's sporting events, keep your perspective. Don't take it too seriously. It's only a game. During a Little League baseball game, if the umpire calls your child out on strikes, don't groan, don't rant, don't swallow your tongue. Don't question the umpire's eyesight, integrity or ancestry. He is probably a parent, too. Don't let your child see Daddy blow his cool and assault the umpire. Remember: A strikeout will not mark your child for life. It will not go on his or her permanent record. When your child gets to heaven, St. Peter will *not* ask his or her batting average. But when that umpire gets to heaven, St. Peter *will* ask him how he got that Louisville Slugger embedded in his head.

Daddy Dearest

A Real Man is mindful of the fragile psyches of his children. For example, when one of his teen-ager's little friends tele-

Louisville Slugged

phones but his teen-ager is answering a call of nature, a Real Man says, "He/she can't come to the phone right now." A Real Man does *not* say, "He/she is on the pot right now."

The Good Humor Man

A Real Man humors his mother, no matter how old he is. For example, she may remind you to "drive slowly today—the streets are wet" or "dress warm—it's cold out." At such times you may be sorely tempted to blurt out: "Mother, *please*! I'm a grown man. I will be fifty-one years old in July. I have grown children. I have fought in a major U.S. war, crossed the Atlantic on a catamaran and wrestled a crocodile. I am the CEO of a major corporation. I have been on the cover of *Time* magazine. I have an *ulcer* that is old enough to know to 'drive slowly' and 'dress warm.' *Please* treat me like an adult."

Don't.

Play the role of Sonny Boy. Indulge her maternal need to fuss and fret. No matter how old a man is, he will always be a little boy to his mother. The relationship between mother and son is forever. A man of eighty who has a mother of one hundred is still a little boy:

Eighty-year-old son: "Well, Mom. I'm glad you called. It was good to talk with you. But I gotta go now. My wing of the nursing home is having Paper Crafts Night, and I'm in charge of the supplies."

One hundred-year-old mother: "Don't run with the scissors."

8

REACH OUT, REACH OUT
AND TOUCH NO ONE

A Real Man is polite on the telephone. When his phone rings, a Real Man does not answer with a growl that would indicate to the caller that he or she has interrupted the Real Man in the middle of (1) a heart transplant or (2) sex or (3) hibernating in a cave for the winter.

When the phone rings a Real Man answers amiably, cheerfully, as if it might—just might—be Kim Basinger finally returning his calls.

If he has Call Waiting, he doesn't keep the first caller dangling when he gets a second call. And he doesn't phone someone and then promptly put that person on hold. This happened to us at NAGD just the other day. We received a call, and in a matter of seconds, the caller put us on hold. In fact, we are *still* on hold, still listening to the soft, soothing "hold" music in our ear. We have listened to the instrumental version of "You're Having My Baby" so many times that in the more-liberal states we are qualified to be an ob-gyn.

Double Talk

A Real Man also does not try to hold simultaneous conversations with someone on the phone and someone in person. The person on the phone does not care to hear one side of a conversation between you and a colleague, a neighbor or a family member. It's like watching only half of a table tennis game. All ping and no pong.

9

DURESS FOR SUCCESS

As Americans moved from the country to the city through the generations, the office replaced the farm as a workplace. As a result, where once the Real Man grew potatoes, now he grows memos. Where once the Real Man worked under the sun, now he works under fluorescent lights. Where once the Real Man went to bed at night worried about questions such as whether the rain would fall, whether the soil would be fertile and whether insects would eat the crops, now he goes to bed at night worried about questions such as whether he is contributing sufficiently to the company's success, whether he is living up to his fullest potential as a dedicated employee and whether anyone has noticed that in the last ten years he has taken home $20,000 worth of office supplies.

But whether on the farm or in the office, the etiquette is the same: Consider the feelings of others, be sensitive to their ambitions. Remember that the workplace is a competitive arena. Chances for advancement are finite. When colleagues are given a promotion or some honor that you dearly wanted, be a good loser. Be sincerely happy for them. Congratulate them, slap them on the back. Heartily. Preferably until their fillings fly out.

On the other hand, if you are the one who is given a promotion or some honor that your colleagues dearly wanted, be a good winner. Don't gloat. Offer your colleagues encouragement. Offer your colleagues consolation. If all else fails, offer your colleagues a box of rubber bands, a ream of typing paper and a stapler of their choice.

You have plenty more.

If you are having a bad day at home, don't take it out on your colleagues. For example, let's say that your teen-age son suddenly announces at breakfast that when he grows up he wants to become either a priest or a mass murderer—

whichever gets more publicity. Don't take your frustration out on your colleagues. Your colleagues probably don't even *own* a complete set of Ted Bundy trading cards.

Staff Infection

When attending office staff meetings, always show interest in what your colleagues say. If a colleague is talking or making a presentation, pretend to take notes, even if you are merely doodling pictures of your colleague as he or she might look as Mr. or Mrs. Potato Head.

Don't use a staff meeting as an opportunity to curry the favor of superiors.

Don't bring a Walkman.

Don't bring a date.

Party Hardly

A Real Man is careful of how he deports himself at office social functions because he knows that no matter how much fun he has at the office party on Friday night, come Monday morning he will have to face those same people

Mr. Potato Head Presents

again. This generally means ruling out any party activity that involves his boss's boss's boss's wife, a hall closet and any side dish made from cabbage.

Question: Even if the coleslaw was her idea?

Answer: *Especially* if the coleslaw was her idea.

Famous Last Words

In the workplace, a Real Man refers to his female colleagues as "women," not as "chicks" or "babes." Generally, this rule can be broken by Colonel Sanders or Dr. Spock.

10

PRAISE THE LORD AND PASS THE PEPSI

The Screen Is Silver, Silence Is Golden

There is proper men's etiquette for the movie theater, too. Don't arrive after the film has begun; don't kick the seat in front of you; don't lay claim to both arm rests unless your date is the Venus de Milo.

Also, don't take a seat in the middle of an aisle filled with other people if you are outfitted with (1) a forty-two-ounce soft drink and (2) a bladder whose capacity is described, in urological terms, as "demitasse."

Above all else, don't talk out loud to the characters on the screen. They can't hear you. But everyone else in the theater can. And they don't want to listen to you calling out:

"Look out, Clint! Behind you!" and "Don't open that door, Arnold!" and "Duck, Sigourney! He's got a gun!"

And pay attention. Keep up with the plot. So that you don't have to ask out loud: "Huh? What'd she say just then?" and "Who is *he*?" and "Hey, was that a breast just then? It was, wasn't it?! Look! There's another one! Boy, that Madonna sure can act!"

Such rudeness can have tragic consequences. One time we here at NAGD were at a movie when a guy in the audience kept talking out loud to the screen and asking dumb questions. Eventually, after several of these irritating outbursts, Miss Manners rose from her seat a few rows up, stormed down the aisle and stabbed the offender with a calligraphy pen. She later used the pen to write a tasteful note of condolence to the man's widow.

Matthew, Mark, Luke and Harpo

In church, while the minister delivers his sermon he appreciates a spirit-filled "amen!" or "hallelujah!" from a Real Man now and then, but for the most part, church etiquette is the same as theater etiquette—be quiet while the minister reads from the Bible. Don't shout: "Keep your eye on him, Abel!" and "No, Lot! Don't let your wife look back!" and "Whoa! Don't go to sea today, Jonah!"

11

"AHHHHH'S" AND OWES

Readin', Writin' and Reminiscin'

At a high school reunion, while you are catching up on what
has happened with your old classmates in the years since
you last saw them, show as much interest in their lives as
you want them to show in yours. "Ahhhhh" and "ewwwww"
when they show you snapshots of the people dear to them
(their spouse, their children, their grandchildren) before
you drag out snapshots of the people dear to *you* (your wife,
your children, your prostate surgeon).

Also remember that if your wife accompanies you to the
reunion but did not attend your high school, she is apt to
feel superfluous and left out of all the reminiscing. So find
ways to make her feel included in your conversations, to

make them relevant to her. But there is a wrong way and a right way:

> Wrong way: "Hey, Tom, do you remember that time you and I double-dated with those two long-legged, gorgeous nymphomaniacs, neither of whom was my lovely wife Donna here?"

> Right way: "Hey, Tom, do you remember that time you and I did *not* double-date with those two long-legged, gorgeous nymphomaniacs, neither of whom was my lovely wife Donna here?"

At reunions people inevitably exaggerate. They embellish their affluence, their influence, their job title. Fine for them. A Real Man is too polite to express any skepticism to them. And as for his own accomplishments, a Real Man is too secure, too modest to stoop to exaggeration. He knows that he has no need to lie about his job. He knows that he has no need to embellish his accomplishments. He knows that wearing a simple name tag that reads thusly will suffice:

[his name]
POPE

Above all else, a Real Man does not relive the good old high school times, however memorable they might have been, if acting them out involves lowering (1) his pants and (2) the window of a '66 Chevy.

Subtract Line 34 from Rodent 32

When all those years of claiming your children's hamsters as dependents on your income tax return lead to an audit by the IRS, three rules of etiquette apply—(1) don't fall to your knees and cling begging to the auditor's leg* and (2) compliment the auditor's cattle prod and (3) stand up when the pit bulldogs enter the room.

(*By substituting "warden's," "judge's" and "bride's" for "auditor's," this rule also applies to parole hearings, court trials and wedding nights.)

Imbibed Embellishment

12

IN OTHER WORDS

Come Heck or High Water

We here at NAGD know of a man who went home one day only to find his brand new house mysteriously sinking into a swamp. And this was the second time that week that it had happened! As the man watched his house slipping from view, his family was huddled on the roof, clinging to the chimney. On the porch, alligators were snapping at the Avon lady. His real estate agent paddled by and waved cheerfully.

Well, we here at NAGD can assure you that this poor, put-upon man reacted to all this misfortune with a string of profanity—hand-me-down expletives that were already threadbare when he learned them at (or across) his father's knee.

Understandable, you might say. But hardly inevitable, we here at NAGD say. A Real Man minds his mouth, even in an era when expletives punctuate sentences like commas. Why? For one reason, some people are offended by such words. For another reason, expletives that once were used sparingly and with deliberation—for effect or shock value—are so common now that they have lost their impact. Many people don't even notice such words anymore. People have become desensitized to them. Expletives have become the cereal filler in the wiener of communication.

Mathematically, the impact of an expletive is inversely proportional to the frequency of its use. This can be stated in the following equation:

$$I = \frac{1}{F}$$

where "I" is the impact that an expletive has upon people and "F" is the frequency of its use (Our thanks to Jeff in NAGD's Department of Advanced Etiquette Mathematics and Naughty Words for formulating this equation.).

Expletives fall into two main categories—profanity, relating to religion; and obscenity, relating to the human body and the functions thereof. But religion hasn't changed much in ages (and the rock thereof), and the human body hasn't changed much since our nephew went to Sweden and came back buttoning his clothes on the left side.

Thus America's obscenities are obsolete—obsolenities.

So perhaps it's time that we Real Men tossed out all our trite old expletives and whipped up a new batch—some that are personal and relevant to each individual. Perhaps each of us Real Men should keep a diary—pardon us, *journal*— for a month, jotting down the words for all the things and concepts and actions that we hate, words that are truly worthy of serving as personal expletives.

For example, for one man it might be words such as "liberal Democrat" or "rap music" or "commuting." For another man it might be words such as "smoking prohibited" or "inflation" or "Rush Limbaugh."

Regardless, with practice these two men could substitute these fresh, personal expletives for the hackneyed, second-hand expletives in their vocabulary. As in:

First man: "Liberal Democrat it all, Jim! That rap music dog of yours has gotten into my commutin' trash cans again!"

Second man: "Well, Rush Limbaugh *you*, buddy!"

Of Mice and Mince

However, Real Men are also careful not to euphemize too much. We here at NAGD maintain that Real Men are sensitive to the feelings of others, especially others who face extra difficulties in life. But as men who grew up calling a spade a spade—not a "foot-activated earth-excavating implement"—Real Men are wary of phraseology that is so hypersensitive as to be silly. Real Men are willing to call the poor "economically disadvantaged." But they wonder where such a trend might lead. Will the short come to be called "vertically deficient" and the bald "follicularly deprived"? Will single people become "nuptially impaired"? Will the fat be called "bulk blessed," the old be called "age endowed" and the wrinkled be called "epidermally surplused"?

It's enough to make a Real Man wish that he were "metabolically disenfranchised."

13

MIND YOUR P'S & Q'S
AT A & P

Yes, Real Men do shop for groceries. For them, grocery-shopping is the twentieth-century equivalent of hunting. True, a cart and a list may seem sissy substitutes for the spear and club of yore. Wheeling past the meat counter may not compare with tiptoeing stealthily through a forest or over a prairie in search of prey. But at least in the supermarket a Real Man can still experience the primitive satisfaction of singling out his quarry, stalking it and, springing with lightning reflexes, bringing down that rogue slab of bacon. But the Real Man must be quick: He knows that a slab of bacon can be savage when cornered or wounded, and he is also careful to keep an eye out for its mate.

Question: You mean...?

Answer: Yes—a carton of eggs.

While shopping, a Real Man observes certain rules of etiquette. He does not get in the "12 items or less" express line if he has twenty items. He does not get in the "cash only" line if he has a third-party, out-of-state check. He writes out his check except for the amount and has his ID ready *before* the total is rung up. A Real Man does not park his cart in the middle of an aisle, blocking the aisle and thus causing other shoppers inconvenience. A Real Man would not leave his car parked in the middle of a street, and the same rules of common sense and common courtesy should apply in a supermarket aisle.

Such breaches of etiquette are all too common. Which is why we here at NAGD think that the time has come for The Shopping Police. These would be specially trained crack squads of people who would dress in plain clothes and patrol the aisles of our supermarkets and discount department stores. When they witnessed an etiquette violation—such as leaving a cart in the middle of an aisle—they would issue a citation to the offender. These citations would be payable by cash or by cents-off coupons. After the third conviction, an offender would be sentenced to thirty days sacking groceries or, if the offender is a man, to thirty days stocking the feminine hygiene aisle.

14

MOVING VIOLATIONS

High Anxiety

We here at NAGD are only too aware that flying in an airplane can be a frightening, stress-inducing ordeal. It is hurtling through the sky at five hundred miles per hour at an altitude of thirty thousand feet while strapped into a thin metal tube. Meanwhile, sitting beside you is some stranger reading out loud from the latest issue of *Outgoing Young White Anglo-Saxon Protestant Businessman's Weekly.* But in your anxiety do not forget your manners: Don't kick the seat bottom of the passenger in front of you. Likewise, notify the person sitting behind you before you put your seat back into the "Hi! I'm here to have my teeth cleaned" position.

Don't carry on articles that are too large to fit into the overhead luggage bins and require you to block the aisle while you futilely push and jam. Such items include military duffel bags, guitar cases and any member of the Cartwright family larger than Little Joe.

Strife in the Fast Lane

We here at NAGD realize that we men have a special relationship with cars and with driving. Personally, we here at NAGD have openly wept upon parting with a car we had owned a long time. The car is one of the few remaining places where a man is an independent agent, sovereign, in control. Control is important to us men. We like to pretend that we still have some. When a man gets behind the wheel, he is riding tall in the saddle, free to ride the asphalt prairie, yee-hah.

But driving is also one of the few social situations where etiquette is essential, where rudeness can be fatal. And driving presents so many opportunities for rudeness. We here at NAGD calculate that there are fifty-seven ways to be rude while driving, not counting popping wheelies in a funeral procession.

Driving can bring out the worst in people. A man who is Peter Polite in the home and office may become Randy Rude behind the wheel. He may fail to give turn signals; he may drive thirty-five miles per hour in the fast lane and seventy in school zones; he may stop his car in traffic to talk with a buddy on the sidewalk; he may create gridlock; he may veer across four lanes of traffic, his car swerving unpredictably like a Scud missile with a "have a nice day" sticker.

Question: Are such men inconsiderate and arrogant?

Answer: Yes, although we here at NAGD grudgingly accept the term "humility impaired."

A man may make a statement with what he drives, but he makes a bigger statement with *how* he drives. A Real Man does not want that statement to be: "Look at me—I'm a jerk."

So a Real Man gives turn signals. When changing lanes, when passing, when turning corners, when entering and exiting the flow of traffic. He knows that the road is no place for surprises. If a Real Man wants to surprise someone, he picks up the check for lunch.

And a Real Man does not drive too slowly in the fast lane. The man who does so controls the lives of those behind him who want to go faster ("OK, everyone behind me, Simon says: 'second gear!'").

We here at NAGD would suggest that Real Men use this little ruse that we use to make driving more personal and to motivate us to drive courteously: As we drive, we imagine that every car around us is being driven by someone dear to us—our family members, our friends, our VCR repairman. Would we be rude and reckless to our VCR repairman? Not if we want to get our VCR repaired in time to watch that special collector's-edition tape of *Ernest Passes a Stone* this weekend.

Strife in the Fast Lane

No Monopoly on the Park Place

A Real Man does not park in a fire lane, a no-parking zone or a handicapped zone just to save himself a few steps. Real Men may be afraid to dance, express their innermost feelings and make a commitment, but they aren't afraid to walk.

A Real Man does not park on a street when a driveway or parking lot is available. He knows that streets—like supermarket aisles, airliner aisles and most of the ties in his closet—are too narrow to begin with.

When a Real Man does park his car on the street, he checks to be sure his car is close to the curb. On a lot he makes sure his car is parked between the painted lines. And he *never* straddles his car across two or even three spaces just to prevent other cars from parking near his and dinging his doors. Maybe when The Shopping Police get off work at the supermarket, they can go out to the parking lot and use cutting torches to remove those parts of cars that extend beyond the borders of a single space.

Question: What could The Shopping Police do with those parts?

Answer: Dump them on the lawns of people who litter.

Dead Ahead

When a Real Man rides on public transportation such as buses, trains and subways, he should not talk to people who are not actually there beside him at the time, such as members of the Cabinet, Larry King and anyone who is deceased.

Overdrive

Like our fathers before us and their fathers before them, when we men participate in family trips, we tend to regard the driver's seat as *our* personal domain. But it wouldn't kill us to pry our fingers off the steering wheel once in a while and let someone else drive. We here at NAGD have tried this and can promise you that as a passenger you will see the passing world from a new perspective and notice scenery that you never had a chance to see as the driver ("Gee, I never realized that Kansas has all this wheat.").

Double-Parked

When we men are behind the wheel, we also tend to drive great distances without stopping. This tendency can be traced back to America's pioneer days, when men pushed their covered wagons relentlessly westward, stopping only at nightfall, when, having no headlights, they had to stop and hastily cut down enough trees to build a Holiday Inn.

Today's man typically refuses to stop driving until (1) he reaches his destination or (2) he runs out of gas or (3) the other people in the car band together and actually hijack the car. A week after they get back home, they remember that he is still locked in the trunk with the souvenir cheese from Wisconsin.

Don't let this happen to you, men. Stop the car once in a while. Your kids would like to stretch their legs. Your wife would like to visit the rest room. And they *all* would like to eat between oil changes.

Two by Two

Traveling with a companion—a wife or a friend—can be a great strain on a marriage or a friendship. Traveling is an endless chain of details—maintaining a schedule, negotiating airports, enduring the physical challenges of flying, riding, driving, walking, waiting in lines, sleeping in unfamiliar beds, etc. All of which makes etiquette crucial. Consider your companion. And be willing to compromise. For example, if you and your travel companion are in New York City, and you want to see the Rockettes whereas your companion wants to see Grant's Tomb, don't insist that your companion see the Rockettes at the exclusion of Grant's Tomb. If there is not time for the two of you to do both together, divide and conquer—you go see the Rockettes while your companion goes to see Grant's Tomb. Then that night the two of you can exchange experiences—you can act out the dance routines, and your companion can act out being dead.

Bye, American

When traveling in foreign countries, don't be impatient with the natives if they don't speak English, and don't expect people on the other side of the world to do things the way we do in America. After all, if they did, would you even bother to go? Don't make fun of foreigners' clothing, currency, religion or customs, although we here at NAGD have talked it over and agreed that it is socially acceptable, after you get back to America, to cup your hand over your mouth and snicker softly.

Be polite to street urchins and street vendors. They may beg you for money, they may ask you to buy worthless trinkets, they may be reluctant to take "no" for an answer. Don't be rude. Have compassion. Count your blessings. Remember that we in America spend more money on video movie rentals in a week than those people earn in a month.

Question: Have you rented Kenneth Branagh's version of Shakespeare's "Henry V" yet?

Answer: No. Is Bob Denver in that one?

Bear in mind that as an overseas traveler you may be some foreigners' first American—the representative of a great, almost mythical country that they have only dreamed about. They may see you as Teddy Roosevelt, Jesse James and Paul Bunyan rolled into one very traveled-in suit. So stand tall, Real Man, carry yourself with quiet dignity, and once in a while run through their restaurants shouting, "Charge!" "Reach for the sky!" and "Tim-berrrrrr!" It'll cost you nothing, and it will brighten a lot of dreary foreign lives.

15

SERVE FROM THE LEFT, SPILL FROM THE RIGHT

Few situations reveal deficiencies in a Real Man's social skills more than eating does. It is ironic that the same man whose hands can play a guitar, build a ship in a bottle and perform magic tricks can't quite come to grips with a knife and fork. Considering how much time we spend eating and drinking, you'd think that we would have gotten the hang of it by now. But as we here at NAGD know only too well, after some men have eaten a meal, they look like a living geography book—Swiss chard between their teeth, French fries in their lap, Russian dressing on their shirt front, Old Milwaukee on their breath.

Lapses in a man's social skills at the table are most likely to occur under these two circumstances:

(1) when dining with someone to whom you would like to appear suave and well-bred—a fiancee's parents, a prospective employer or anyone who is addressed as "Your Highness," "Your Holiness" or "Tipper." And the harder you try to do everything right while eating, the more likely that the demons in your subconscious are to strike, causing you suddenly to begin eating mashed potatoes with your fingers or flipping spoonfuls of fruit cocktail at your future mother-in-law.

(2) in a five-star restaurant. The fancier the setting, the more likely that you will spill food, use the wrong eating implement, or, while trying to spear a bean with your fork, launch it off the plate and into the air like some sort of intercontinental ballistic legume.

Personally, we here at NAGD have gotten so rattled while eating at a fancy restaurant—what with trying to be suave and deft and use the correct fork and chew without biting our tongue—that eventually we have had to summon the maitre d' and ask that a telephone be brought to our table.

Then we suavely and deftly used the correct finger to dial the nearest Domino's and order a pizza.

Here are a few basic eating tips:

If you have a beard or mustache, be very careful when eating a juicy sandwich or hamburger. Sometimes cruel people will even serve you a juicy hamburger just to watch you get most of it in your beard. So wipe your mouth with your napkin frequently. After every bite would not be too often. But the best policy is to ask the waiter or hostess to put the hamburger into a blender, liquefy it and bring it to you in a glass. A glass of fries on the side is optional.

Don't spit seeds or pits at your plate. Dunk basketballs, not doughnuts. Never reach over and spear food from the plate of your fellow diners. Military historians now think that this is how the Spanish-American War began—during a state dinner the Spanish ambassador reached over and took a forkful of fish off the American ambassador's plate. By the time the second course was served, the two countries were at war.

Blendy's Old-Fashioned Hamburgers

Remember that these are finger foods: corn on the cob, olives, bread. And these are not: soup, Jell-O.

Don't be rude to your waiter. Don't bark at him. Don't act superior or condescending (That's *his* job.). Granted, your waiter is there to wait on you, to serve your every need, but he's also a human being. It may not be his fault that your order is slow in being filled or that the restaurant is out of your favorite dish. Lord knows he didn't *want* to become a waiter. For all you know he wanted to be a brain surgeon, but he couldn't find a hospital that pays in tips. So be polite to him. Because waiters have feelings, too. Because you would want to be treated with respect if the tables were turned.

Question: Why else?

Answer: Because if you tick the waiter off, in the kitchen he will spit in your water glass.

16

FROM THE CRADLE TO THE GRAVE

Some miscellaneous etiquette stuff that we had left over:

When Attending Lamaze Class: Don't flirt.

Things not to Pop: Knuckles, gum, towels, tests, pimples, condoms, bra straps.

Oedipus Reeks: If the fumes from your cologne or aftershave set off smoke alarms, consider switching to something milder. Like kerosene.

Speedo Meter: Never wear swim trunks that are smaller than the shadow cast by your belly.

Bumper Stickers and T-Shirts: Don't wear on your bumper or chest any printed message that you wouldn't want to recite to your granny.

Bathroom Etiquette: Never use the bidet to try out a new fishing lure.

Golf Etiquette: Always offer to let the following play through—your elders, your boss, anyone whose golf bag includes more rifles than woods.

Doctor's Waiting Room Etiquette: Don't ask other patients to play "Guess my disease."

Dating Etiquette: Don't begat and be gone.

Hot Tub Etiquette: Don't bring your snorkel.

Nudist Camp Etiquette: Don't point.

When Attending a Funeral: Don't start "the wave."

PAST PERFECT

Rules of etiquette have been in print for centuries. Here are some from days gone by:

George Washington himself served up this heapin' helping of table etiquette:

"Eat not with greediness."

"Lean not on the table, neither find fault with what you eat."

"Drink nor talk with your mouth full."

"Cleanse not your teeth at table with napkin or fork, but if others do it let it be done with a picktooth."

"Kill no vermin as fleas, lice, etc., in the sight of others."

A century later, Victorian sexologist Orson Squire Fowler offered this advice to gentlemen concerning when a marriage should be consummated:

"Let the young husband's sexual approaches be so gradual, from day to day and week to week, as never to shock the bride's modesty till it is supplanted by her own spontaneous passion. This should take months, perhaps a year."

In France in the mid-nineteenth century an etiquette book dictated that:

"A gentleman walking should always wear gloves, this being one of the characteristics of good breeding" and "avoid swearing. An oath is but the wrath of a perturbed spirit."

"Avoid displaying excess of jewelry. Nothing looks more effeminate upon a man."

"Never be without a handkerchief" but "avoid extreme patterns, styles and colours" and "avoid using it too much."

Meanwhile, across the channel an English almanac of the period had this to say about male manners:

"Punctuality is essential to the character of a Gentleman."

"Avoid argument with ladies."

"Never refuse a pinch of snuff."

And a book on dance etiquette published in France in 1623 had these instructions on how to execute, rather narcissistically, "The Bow to Salute a Lady":

"This is performed in exactly the same manner as that for greeting a lord, except that, after kissing his own hand, the Cavalier should then kiss the lady."

The Dutch scholar Erasmus was plain-spoken in his *De Civilitate*—an influential treatise on etiquette written in 1530:

"It is boorish to wipe one's nose on one's cap or clothing; to do so on one's sleeve or forearm is for fishmongers....If, in clearing your nose with two fingers, some matter falls on the ground, it should be immediately ground under foot."

"Turn away when spitting to avoid spitting on or spraying someone. If any disgusting matter is spat onto the ground, it should, as I have said, be ground under foot lest it nauseate someone."

"It is impolite to be continually scratching one's head in front of others just as it is unsightly to scratch the rest of the body."

"Do not throw bones or similar left-overs under the table to litter the floor."

"Clothing too short to conceal, when one is bending over, those parts that modesty requires to be hidden, is distasteful in every society."

"There are some who lay down the rule that a boy should refrain from breaking wind by constricting his buttocks. But it is no part of good manners to bring illness upon yourself while striving to appear 'polite.' If you may withdraw, do so in private. But if not, then in the words of the old adage, let him cover the sound with a cough."

Missed Manners

EPILOGUE

Whither Goest Thou, Earl (Still Not His Real Name)?
With that sage advice from Erasmus, we here at the National
Academy of Gentlemanly Deportment bring to a close this
guidebook of modern etiquette for the primitive man. We feel
no need to examine the subject further because (1) we have
thoroughly covered all aspects of male manners and (2) we
have spent all the money that Mrs. Earl gave us.

We hope that in these few pages we have provided some
useful and valid guidelines to help improve the etiquette of
Earl (still not his real name) and other men—including ourselves here at NAGD. We hope that we have shown that with
only ten percent more consideration of others, men and
women alike can have a world that is ninety percent better.
We hope that we have shown that Real Men belch downwind,

always mindful of their "corrupt fumosytye," that man's primitive side and proper etiquette can coexist, that the American male can be manly to the marrow and still be courteous, and that all of us men should pay at least as much attention to our manners as we do to the Dallas Cowboys cheerleaders.

Thus enlightened we—the new breed of Real Men—can march proudly and politely into the twenty-first century with our head held high, our shoulders back, our mind open and our fly closed.

And as our fellow Real Men march toward the new millennium, they can be assured that we here at NAGD will continue to be ever vigilant. Tireless and imbued with fierce and unflagging devotion to duty, we will monitor the ever-changing state of masculine etiquette. First thing tomorrow. Because today we are going fishing.

After all, we have a new fully rigged bass boat to try out.

Question: Does it have the optional sonar fish-finder?

Answer: Yes, it does, and thank you so much for asking.